PIANO · VOCAL · GUITAR

THE HISTORY OF ROCK
THE LATE 50s

M000159810

THE TEEN REIGNED SUPREME
AND ROCK AND ROLL WAS HERE TO STAY...
FROM AMERICAN BANDSTAND TO THE
TEEN IDOLS TO DOO WOP'S CLOSE HARMONIES

COVER BACKGROUND: WESTLIGHT

ISBN #0-7935-0019-2

Hal Leonard Publishing Corporation
7777 West Bluemound Road P.O. Box 13819 Milwaukee, WI 53213

CHRONOLOGICAL CONTENTS

ALPHABETICAL CONTENTS

THE HISTORY OF ROCK
THE LATE 50s

MANY CITE 1957 AS A PIVOTAL YEAR. AFTER ALL, IT WAS THE YEAR SPUTNIK WAS LAUNCHED. HOWEVER, IN ROCK ANNALS, IT WAS PIVOTAL BECAUSE IT WAS THE YEAR AMERICAN BANDSTAND WAS LAUNCHED. THIS SHOW WAS, IN A SENSE, A VICTORY FOR TEENAGERS AND FOR ROCK. TEENS NOW HAD THEIR OWN PROGRAM THAT FEATURED THEIR STYLES AND THEIR MUSIC AND SPOKE DIRECTLY TO THEM. FOR THE FIRST TIME IN MODERN HISTORY, TEENS HAD BECOME AN ECONOMIC AND TREND-SETTING FORCE.

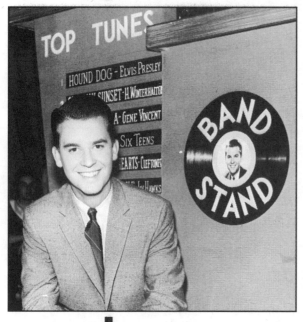

AN EARLY SHOT (1956) OF DICK CLARK BEFORE AMERICAN BANDSTAND WENT NATIONAL.

Bandstand started as a local show on WFIL in Philadelphia where DJ Dick Clark played pop records and used film clips of artists supplied by the record companies, managers, or even their publishers (the forerunner of MTV?). The studio was near a high school and the students would drop in to watch the filming and often start to dance spontaneously. So, dancing on-camera on the show just evolved naturally, with the "regulars" becoming local stars.

The show went national on August 5, 1957 with the "regulars" dancing, Clark playing records (the first being Jerry Lee Lewis' "Whole Lotta Shakin'") and interviewing the on-screen artists, Tony Williams, and the Chordettes (see DOO WOP, DOO WOP), who then lip-synced their tunes. The show was seen by an estimated 20 million viewers weekly; its effect on the teen world was dramatic. Clark in his button-down suit was a cooler, more contained, less threatening promoter of rock than Alan Freed, with his emotion-tinged championing of the true roots of rock: R&B. Rock was considered very threatening – churches banned it, parents hated it because they couldn't understand it, major record companies didn't want to change for it (even though they were losing money to the independent companies because of it), and members of the Senate thought it was a factor in juvenile delinquency. Nevertheless, Dick Clark made rock acceptable to the nation.

Clark and the *American Bandstand* "regulars" and staff started a great many fads, created many new dances, were a force behind a large number of hits and the star-making machinery for a multitude of artists. Numerous stars owed their popularity to their exposure on *Bandstand*. For instance, when Clark broke Connie Francis' tune "Who's Sorry Now" on *Bandstand*, she was wavering between taking a scholarship to New York University and continuing trying to get a hit after five failed records. The first of the young teen idols, Fabian, Bobby Rydell, Paul Anka and Frankie Avalon all made their debuts on *Bandstand*. The audience for Chuck Berry and Jerry Lee Lewis widened considerably following their *Bandstand* appearances.

BANDSTANDERS BOPPING. NOTE THE GIRLS DANCING WITH GIRLS, AND THE GIRLS' HEAVY SOCKS, SWEATER SETS AND LACE COLLARS – ALL TO BECOME NATIONAL FADS.

A *Bandstand* regular, Bobby Darin played six instruments and could perform stylistically across the board – from rock to the current nightclub standards at the Copa. His hit, "Splish Splash" (written on a dare after he boasted to top DJ Murray the "K," that he could write a song on any subject. Murray said, "Okay, write a song with the line 'splish, splash, I was taking a bath.'") was premiered at a Dick Clark record hop. The kids went so wild over the recording that Clark was forced to repeat it twice before the end of the evening.

The first big dance craze that *Bandstand* broke was the Bop. Clark spotted two teens visiting from Los Angeles doing a different kind of fast dance and had them teach it to the "regulars." Within a week, all the people on the show were "bopping," and before long it was a nation-wide rage. Then, in '57, the Stroll was introduced on the show. In the Stroll, dancers formed two lines – boys facing girls – then the couple at the end would "stroll" down the line with a group of intricate steps, joining the line at the end.

The king of Stroll was singer Chuck Willis, who introduced the dance on *Bandstand* to the tune of "C.C. Rider." However, Dick Clark's chance remark to Nat Goodman, manager of the group, the Diamonds, that "...there was no specific 'Stroll' song," sparked the Diamonds to commission three different songwriters to come up with a song. They took the best, and by Christmas of '57 they had a hit entitled "The Stroll."

BANDSTAND REGULARS DOING THE STROLL (WITH DICK CLARK, CENTER REAR).

TEEN IDOLS

This was the dawn of rock and roll packaging. Up until the late '50s, rock artists had, for the most part, come to the public as pretty unique packages unto themselves. Presley, Haley, Berry, Lewis, Richard and Domino were all great musicians, terrific showmen and characters of a sort. Yes, some of their managers/record producers/publishers did have a hand in *molding* them, but these artists were exemplary musicians as well as having a sense of style and visual impact.

THE DIAMONDS (COURTESY OF RHINO RECORDS)

So, when it was obvious that rock was here to stay, it was time to cash in on the teen idols, and Philadelpia (Bandstandland) became the most fertile place to begin. First came Francis Thomas Avallone and Robert Louis Ridarelli, whose parents encouraged them as kids by showcasing them constantly at a local private club. Francis, who also played trumpet, became Frankie Avalon, did a number of national TV shows as a child and then joined a local Philly band, Rocco and The Saints. Robert, dubbed Bobby Rydell by famed bandleader Paul Whiteman, joined Avalon as a drummer for the group and they gigged together for a couple of years.

Meanwhile, two songwriters Bob Marcucci and Pete DeAngelis had formed Chancellor Records. Marcucci was the businessman, the promoter; De Angelis was more the musician and had jammed occasionally with Avalon. At the inception of the company, Avalon auditioned for them and cut two tunes, both flops. Then he cut "De De Dina," joking around and holding his nose to get a pinched sound. That sound was great, according to Marcucci, and in 1958 the song was Avalon's, as well as the company's, first hit. Avalon followed with several more hits, the 1959 #1 hit, "Venus," was his biggest.

It wasn't Avalon's tunes that made the impact as much as his sex appeal. He was a teen idol and his appearances on *Bandstand* drove the girls wild. Marcucci's next discovery was even more of a "package," however, than Avalon. Legend has it that Marcucci stopped on a Philadelphia street to help a cop who was ill. When Marcucci met the cop's son, Fabian Forte, he was struck by his resemblance to Elvis Presley – high shiny black hair, olive coloring, and a slight sneer on his lips. The problem was, he couldn't sing. Marcucci took care of that with two years of singing lessons, speaking lessons and special etiquette and grooming. He ran full page ads in the music trades, and Fabian (no last name) was released on Marcucci's Chancellor Records with his first hit "Turn Me Loose."

There were other teen idols who came along with genuine talent. The very precocious Paul Anka was writing and performing by the age of 14. At 16, he had his first big hit with "Diana" in 1957, hit his stride with "Lonely Boy" in '59 and had a multitude of hits thereafter. "Lonely Boy" was a very personal song: At 18, Anka was leaving his teen yeras, his mother was dying and he was struggling to become comfortable with success. Anka was unique in the late '50s, one of the few performers who wrote and sang his own material.

RAUNCHY ROCK

The teen idols were mainly for the girls. It's estimated that teen spending was $9.5 billion in 1958, a major percentage being spent by girls. Girls formed enormous followings and were the main reason for the development of the first teen merchandising efforts with shirts, lunch boxes, book covers, pencils, anything with the artists' image on it. However, there was a harder, sometimes darker, side of rock that appealed mostly to the boys, and showed the influence of rockabilly music, which was definitely dominated by the white, Southern *male* market.

One of these men's men was Jerry Lee Lewis, who made his mark as one of the most energetic, uptempo keyboard rockers of all time. This rockabilly singer from Sun Records (see *History Of Rock – The Birth Of Rock & Roll*) had a tough, gut-wrenching sound and his hit "Great Balls Of Fire" was a perfect description of his frenzied act. He was and is the absolute epitome of rock keyboard sound; no one has ever surpassed his style.

On the guitar side, Duane Eddy changed the course of electric guitar and bass with his instrumental, "Rebel 'Rouser." He played this tune on the newly-released Fender Bass, which looked like an electric guitar, but sounded like an amplified stand-up bass. To this he added electric tremolo (also a new invention) to give the tune an ominous sound. His twangy guitar (melody on the lower strings), along with Link Wray's powerful playing, was to imprint an electric guitar and bass sound on rock that would be the forerunner of heavy metal and the sounds that followed thereafter.

Johnny And The Hurricanes, a purely instrumental group, started out by backing a vocal group at an audition. The singers bombed, but the talent scouts loved the Hurricanes. They had their first hits in '59, most of them (as with "Red River Rock" which was "Red River Valley") based on well-known folk songs. They had a hard-driving rock beat, with a raspy tenor sax and featured wild guitar solos. The respect for their sound was such that in the early '60s they frequently opened for the Beatles when the latter were playing at the Star Club in Hamburg, Germany.

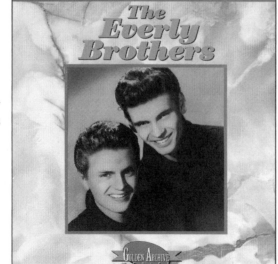

The Champs produced an instrumental, "Tequila," that combined rough-edged rock with the 1958 trend for Latin sounds. This was the group that spawned Glen Campbell and his incredible guitar chops and, later, the talents of Seals and Crofts. As with this group, the solo action in the late '50s was moving away from the saxophone and keyboards toward the guitar.

ALL I HAVE TO DO IS DREAM

Phil and Don Everly were born to perform. Their parents, Ike and Margaret Everly were well-known country singers, and by the time the boys were 9 and 7 respectively, they were performing on their parents' radio show. They were signed to Cadence Records' country/western division in Nashville, where they were fortunate enough to be put with one of the most astute country publishers ever, Wesley Rose. Rose, with performer Roy Acuff, had established a stable of outstanding writers and chalked up many hits on the country charts.

Rose put the Everlys together with a terrific songwriting team, Boudleaux and Felice Bryant, who were established songwriters. The Bryants had a tune "Bye Bye, Love," that had already been rejected 30 times; the Everlys, however, loved it. They recorded it on their first session. Ten days after its release, the song zoomed up the pop charts to number 2 and hit number 1 on the country charts. The Bryants penned the Everlys' "Wake Up Little Susie," which hit number 1, but under duress. The song was banned from many radio stations for being too suggestive, but it hit a responsive chord with any teen who had ever broken curfew.

The Everlys, Rose and their management seemed to be meticulous in their planning. Their recording sessions were known to be arranged and rehearsed well in advance, and featured Nashville's finest session players, including Chet Atkins on guitar and Floyd Cramer on piano. The Bryants tailored songs just for the Everlys' smooth, light, harmonious sound. For three years, the Everlys averaged a top ten hit every four months.

HANG UP MY ROCK AND ROLL SHOES (ONLY THE GOOD DIE YOUNG)

Buddy Holly grew up in Lubbock, Texas, where, in the mid-'50s, the radio fare consisted of pop and country, and they tuned into Shreveport, Louisiana, a thousand miles away, to hear R&B. This particular melange of styles is what molded Holly's rockabilly style.

BUDDY
HOLLY

In the mid-'50s, Holly got his first break as a country artist playing on a local radio station. He added R&B and Presley songs to his act, and as requests grew for rock, he changed the format to appeal to a growing teen audience.

Holly cut several recordings for Decca in 1956. The music trades' reviews were favorable, but the two singles Decca released didn't chart well. Holly was a little too country for the rock stations and too rock for the country stations. However, Holly's manager/producer/writer associate, Norman Petty via a long line of contacts, got a Decca subsidiary, Coral-Brunswick, to take over the masters and release some of the material Holly had recorded at Petty's studio with his group the Crickets.

The Crickets' release "Peggy Sue" (named after drummer Jerry Allison's girlfriend) was high on the charts by November 1957 and joined by "Not Fade Away" in December. "Maybe Baby" was a major hit by March of 1958, and Holly toured and recorded for the next year garnering huge enthusiastic groups of fans as far away as Australia and the U.K. (one well-known fan was Paul McCartney). Holly's fresh guitar style contributed a wealth of technique and licks to future rockabilly players. His hiccuping vocal style – the sound like a *catch* in his throat – became a much-imitated rock vocal technique. He also established some new techniques in the recording studio.*

Alan Freed and later Dick Clark instituted the rock and roll concert tour, usually showcasing a large group of artists. On just such a tour, GAC's *Winter Dance Party* in the Midwest, the Big Bopper joined Buddy Holly (whose band included Waylon Jennings and Tommy Allsup), Ritchie Valens ("La Bamba"), Frankie Sardo, and Dion and The Belmonts. The Big Bopper, former DJ, J.P. Richardson, had written several country hits and had a major hit with "Chantilly Lace," a sexy, but cute teen tune. He wrote in the same rockabilly vein as Holly and Vincent, and had written several country-to-rockabilly hits including the George Jones classic, *White Lightning*.

THE BIG
BOPPER
(COURTESY
OF RHINO
RECORDS)

The tours were grueling at best, and this one was nightmarish most of the time (the drummer suffered frostbite when the heat went out on the bus). On the night of February 2, 1959, Holly

and his group chartered a plane to their next stop so they could sleep in a hotel and take care of their accumulated laundry... luxuries after one-nighters on the bus! The Big Bopper had the flu, so Jennings relinquished his seat on the plane to him. Valens traded places with Allsup on the flip of a coin, provided Allsup could use the Bopper's new sleeping bag on the bus. Shortly after midnight, the plane left the Mason City, Iowa airport and crashed eight miles from the field, killing everyone. This was "the day the music died."**

Like Buddy Holly, it's impossible to speculate what impact Eddie Cochran might have had, had he lived past 21. He was signed to Liberty Records in 1957 on the basis of his successful audition for the film "The Girl Can't Help It." He came to be known as a performer with great guitar chops, and as one whose songs recognized the plights of the teen to their fullest. His classic "Summertime Blues" will never die because its lyric will always be true. He influenced guitarists with his use of a Gretsch semi-acoustic guitar with a humbucker pickup. Cochran was killed in an automobile accident in London in which singer Gene Vincent was severely injured.

*See Buddy Holly – The Golden Anniversary Songbook for more information.

**The line from the classic "American Pie" by Don McLean.

DOO WOP, DOO WOP

Managed by seminal music entrepreneur Buck Ram, the Platters (like the Coasters) were one of the few doo wop groups to have a string of hits in the '50s and the first black group to have a number one hit on the pop charts. Originally, they were purely an R&B group on the indie label, Federal, but Ram insisted to Mercury Records that they become part of the package when they signed his hit group, the Penguins.

The Platters' lead singer, tenor Tony Williams, had a voice as smooth as silk, and Ram had a record promotion person, Jeannie Bennett, who hounded radio stations relentlessly. Their first hit "Only You (And You Alone)" (see History Of Rock – The Birth Of Rock & Roll) stayed on the charts for 28 weeks! Magnificent "Twilight Time," included strings – one of the first R&B hits to do so. The group's last big hit was in 1967, but they amassed 40 chart records, 16 gold singles, and 3 gold albums along the way.

One of rock's first racially-integrated groups, the Del Vikings, was formed at a

Pittsburgh Air Force base. Their first hit, "Come Go With Me," was recorded in the basement of a Pittsburgh disc jockey's house. The *dum dum dum dum dum, dum be doo bee*, became one of the classic doo wop lines.

The Brooklyn group Little Anthony and The Imperials as well as Frankie Lyman and The Teenagers were both discovered in New York by the Valentines' (another doo wop group) manager, Richard Barrett. Their first and biggest of nineteen chart hits was the heart-rending "Tears On My Pillow." Known for his incredible high falsetto, the five-foot four-inch Little Anthony (Anthony Gourdine) got his nickname from DJ Alan Freed. George Goldner, the owner/producer of End Records, carefully coached Gourdine and the group to get the staccato enunciation and deep feeling in their delivery.

Also out of Brooklyn came the Crests, who were prone to singing in the subway (a captive audience). There, they were handed a business card by a woman who encouraged them to see a bandleader, who in turn took them to see George Paxton, owner of Coed Records. Their "Sixteen Candles" was originally the B side of a record, but two important people liked it better than the A side – who could argue with Alan Freed and Dick Clark?

Dion and the Belmonts were Bronx boys (Belmont Avenue is in the Bronx), known for great arrangements and very tight harmony. They broke hearts with "A Teenager In Love" – a lament by Doc Pomus and Mort Shuman – to which every teen could relate. The song started out as an "up" tune, but the record company felt that little "sob" in Dion's voice was better suited to sad songs. Dion went on to fame as a solo act.

The "Get A Job" lyric by the Silhouettes was not teen material, but the beat and doo wops, *yip, yip, yip, yip* and *sha na na*s were great teen dance material. A moment of silence and a stroke on the bass drum made unusual hook in "Book Of Love" by the Monotones. The Tune Weavers' voices imparted delicious melancholy in "Happy, Happy Birthday Baby." These were all one-hit groups, never to be seen again on the charts, but the melodies linger on.

WHY IS EVERYBODY ALWAYS PICKIN' ON ME?

The Coasters began doo wopping on the West Coast as the Robins, recording several hits for Sparks Records, a label owned by the veteran songwriters Leiber and Stoller. When Atlantic Records offered Leiber and Stoller a unique production contract (the first one for independent contractors), two factions within the Robins split and the Coasters were born.

Their sound was tight, their lyric and presentation definitely humorous. In "Young Blood," they're ogling a young woman on the street, when Dad comes along in a basso voice and tells them "what for," but in the song, hope for a tryst springs eternal. Leiber and Stoller's "Yakety Yak" had a great hook, a knock out sax solo by King Curtis, and an even greater commentary of the generation gap.

"Charlie Brown" isn't the guy from Peanuts; he's the cutup everyone knew in school. "Poison Ivy" was the warning about the ever-enduring female who'll make you itch the moment you go after her. There was an obvious thread throughout the Coasters' music – familiar teen feelings and situations.

The Coasters had six top 10 hits and a proportionate amount of R&B chart toppers. They had some of Atlantic Records' (a label whose recordings and marketing were a major influence on R&B and pop music) biggest hits by the time that label celebrated its tenth birthday in 1958.

THE COASTERS IN THE '80S WITH VETERAN PUBLISHER LESTER SILL.

SILLY SONGS – SUCKERS TO BUBBLEGUM

In his extremely detailed book, *The Rockin' '50s*, veteran songplugger Arnold Shaw tells this story of "Lollipop," one of the first examples of what was to be called "bubblegum" music: Songwriter Beverly Ross brought a young black teen named Ronald to Shaw's office with an arrangement of the song. Shaw cut a demo on the tune with Ross and Ronald for $55.00 and sent it to Cadence Records. They liked it so well, they wanted to release it as a master, as did RCA. However, Shaw had 3 problems: Ronald wasn't under contract, he was underage, and he was black and Ross was white and (this was 1958) record companies and DJs didn't dig mixed groups.

While waiting for the solution to these problems, Cadence got antsy. They threatened to record the song with the Chordettes, which they finally did and rushed the records to the DJs. Meanwhile, all problems solved, RCA released the Ruby (Ross) and Ronald version and scooped Cadence's advertising. However, Cadence's promo people hit the DJs and the retail stores faster. "Lollipop" by the Chordettes went to Number 2 on the charts, but could never displace the number one spot of "Tequila."

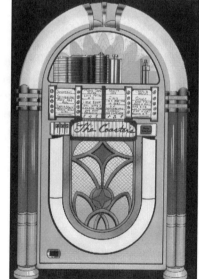

A COASTERS PROMO PIECE

In the '50s, there were silly songs galore from "(How Much Is) That Doggie In The Window" to "Witch Doctor." However most popular of all, "The Purple People Eater," ate its way up to the top of the charts in just 3 weeks. It was recorded by country writer Sheb Wooley who capitalized on the UFO and monster crazes sweeping the country. Its popularity was astonishing – there were even school marching bands performing it as the centerpiece at halftime shows, scribing their own version of the monster purple people eater in marching formation.

Another almost-silly song, "Rockin' Robin," flew up the charts with an excellent dance beat and a flute mimicking bird sounds. This was Bobby Day's only solo hit and Class Records' only hit, but strangely, Day had other hits under various pseudonyms with rock groups and as a writer (he was writer "R. Byrd" on Thurston Harris' "Little Bitty Pretty One."

"Willie And The Hand Jive" was considered a "novelty" tune as well, but its Bo-Diddley type dance beat put it right in the top 10 for Johnny Otis. Otis was a consummate R&B writer and producer who had had hits from 1950 and continued right into the '80s.

THE SOUNDS OF SOUL

R&B, the roots of rock, began making a transition in the late '50s. Jerry Butler's "For Your Precious Love" is considered an R&B milestone. Butler, along with Curtis Mayfield and the Impressions (see *History Of Rock – The Early 60s*), synthesized a different Chicago sound, not the trademark hard-edged workingman's blues, but a combination of gospel, blues, ballads and tight 4-part harmonies (blues and gospel had been on the opposite ends of the musical spectrum in the black communities). The song marks the birth of soul.

Future king of soul, Ray Charles, lost his sight by age 7. Enrolled in the St. Augustine School for the Deaf and the Blind, he learned to read and write music in Braille, scoring for big bands and playing a multitude of instruments. His influences ranged from Chopin to Tatum.

When Charles left school at age 15, he traveled throughout the country making his living playing piano in the smooth, cocktail swing style of Nat "King" Cole. In 1949, he cut his first recording, "Confessin' Blues," and in '51, he had his first top-ten R&B hit. His musical direction turned when he teamed with bluesman, Guitar Slim in New Orleans who worked in a more primitive blues and gospel style. Slim did a recording for Specialty Records (see *History Of Rock – The Birth Of Rock & Roll*), "Things I Used To Do," that sold a million copies and featured Charles as the pianist and arranger.

RAY CHARLES

In December '53, at Charles' request, Ahmet Ertegun, the enthusiastic purveyor of R&B and founder of Atlantic Records, and famed producer Jerry Wexler teamed with Charles in New Orleans to produce his first major hits. Throughout the next six years, Charles had enormous success with an amalgamation of varied styles – R&B, funk, jazz, blues, country, gospel – defining and refining what was about to become "soul music." He sealed his popularity with "What'd I Say" in 1959, a song that was blues and gospel with a slight Latin tinge. Charles sang it as if he was exalting a congregation to sing of the glories of love and the flesh (it was banned on several radio stations). The song made Charles a pop superstar and brought soul into the mainstream for good.

Soulman Jackie Wilson was said to have one of the finest tenor voices in R&B. He had a gospel background and got his first break singing with the Dominoes. His solo debut, "Reet Petite," was written by Berry Gordy, who was to go on to found Motown Records. From the time of his first hit, "Lonely Teardrops," Wilson immediately earned the respect of the musical community for his showmanship and musicianship. His was an uneven career, marred by poor choice of material, spotty marketing and shoddy arrangements, but it lasted almost two more decades to his untimely death.

ROCK AND ROLL IS HERE TO STAY

There were many tunes in this era that were just pure, joyous rock and roll and became rock standards. Danny and Juniors' recording, "At The Hop" (the title was originally "Doing The Bop," but Dick Clark suggested to the writers that the bop was waning, while the record hop was "in") was just such a tune. The group's next hit, "Rock And Roll Is Here To Stay," became a rock anthem at the height of the 1958 rock-bashing period. (The '70s group, Sha Na Na featuring Danny and The Juniors' saxophonist Lennie Baker, covered both of these hits.) Bobby Freeman's "Do You Want To Dance" originally had a "Calypso" beat. It was covered quite differently by the Beach Boys in '65 and in a very sensual version by Bette Midler in 1973. "Sea of Love" was Phil Philips only hit, but it was also a hit for Del Shannon, and for the Honeydrippers, as well as the intense title theme for a late '80s film.

So, a teen generation that had developed its own economic power, changed pop music and the music business was now about to enter the '60s, where they would literally change the world. ∎

ROCK AND ROLL GLOSSARY – THE LATE '50S

AOR: *Album Oriented Rock* – a chart term for album cut airplay on certain broad spectrum FM radio stations.

artists and repertoire: *A&R* The record company personnel responsible for talent acquisition, overseeing their production (and repertoire) and their activities.

ax: A musical instrument.

blast: Having a good time.

bop: n. The bop, a dance, a take off of the swing from the '40s. **v.** To bop, to dance; to go out.

Brill Building: Located at 1619 Broadway in New York City. Home of hundreds of music publishers' offices. Many, many hits were born there.

bugged: To be bothered.

busted: Arrested.

C&W: Country and western music.

chart: A sequential list of hits; a written down musical arrangement (improvised arrangement is called a head arrangement).

chops: A musician's playing technique, ability.

cool: In the '50s, to be hip, in style, okay.

cover: A new recording of a previously recorded song. A common practice in the '50s was for white artists to cover hits by black R&B artists.

crossover: Songs that "cross over" from one chart to another, such as from a country chart to a pop chart.

cut: n. A record; or one song on an album. **v.** To make (cut) a recording.

demo: A demonstration record; used by songwriters and publishers to sell their songs to artists.

dig: To understand, i.e. "Do you dig it?" Late '50s.

distortion devices: For guitar — wah-wah pedal, fuzz tone, reverb, echo, tremolo.

doo wop: A type of close harmony singing, usually with sparse instrumental accompaniment, unique in the use of nonsense syllables as rhythmic background or "punctuation."

dub: n. A copy of the *master*. **v.** To record from a *master*; to insert a new sound, or synchronize one sound with another sound (overdub).

feedback: On a guitar set for feedback, a string will vibrate at a certain pitch so that the sound is picked up by the amplifier and fed back into the string to increase its vibration at that pitch.

flipped out: To really like something/someone, '50s; to be angry, lose one's temper, '70s.

flaked out: Tired.

funk/funky: A rhythm and blues sound, usually lowdown, rhythmic and rough.

fuzztone: A device on a guitar that changes the shape of the soundwave so that the music from the amplifier has a blurred or fuzzy sound. First used by Link Wray.

groove: n. Where music really "clicks" and comes together for the listener, especially rhythmically; as in "in the groove." **v.** To *groove* is to enjoy, be one with (the music or one's lover). **adj.** *Groovy*, in the late '60s/early '70s — anything pleasurable or good.

grounded: Not permitted by parents to drive the car or go out.

head: Someone who takes drugs.

hip: Cool, with it, late '50s.

hook: A repetitive phrase, usually in the chorus, that catches the listener's attention.

jive: n. Slang or colloquial expressions derived from blues slang, used first in the jazz sector and then in '50s rock. **v.** In the early '70s, "don't *jive* me" meant "don't put me on."

licks: Short, melodic musical phrases that sometimes became musical "signatures" for artists.

master: n. Final, completed recording from which copies can be made. **v.** To *master*; to make a master.

mix: To balance all the tracks of a multitrack *master* to bring it to final product status.

MOR: *Middle Of The Road* – a chart term for music, usually ballads, that bridged the gap between easy listening and rock.

overdub: To add parts to and synchronize them in a multitrack recording.

put down: A criticism.

put-on: n. A lie. **v.** Lead someone on.

R&B: *Rhythm and blues*; post World War II black music, replacing the previous appellation of "race" music.

reverb: On guitar, an echo-like sound effect.

riff: A pattern of music, sometimes repetitive; usually played by a rhythm instrument — guitar, bass, drum or keyboards.

rumble: A fight, late '50s.

scene: Where it's happening, late '50s.

shook up: Upset, late '50s.

square: Unhip, uncool, conservative, unknowing in the ways of rock and roll; usually pertaining to one's parents.

standard: A song that continues to remain popular and receive many *covers* over the years.

stoned: High on drugs.

studio musician: A free-lance musician who works primarily in recording studios.

swing: Late '50s, to belong; late '60s, to be sexually permissive; '80s, the music moves.

turn on: n. A *turn-on* – something interesting. **v.** To be *turned on* – to be sexually aroused, or on drugs.

turf: Territory, late '50s.

wah-wah pedal: On guitar, a device that distorts the sound by use of electric currents that vibrate the speakers to emphasize or de-emphasize the middle range of the sound output.

wheels: Car or any motorized transportation.

COME GO WITH ME

Words and Music by C.E. QUICK

Yes, you real-ly nev-er, You nev-er give me a chance.

Come, come, come, come, Come in-to my heart, Tell me, dar-lin',

We will nev-er part; I need you, dar-lin', So come go with

me

me

YOUNG BLOOD

Words and Music by JERRY LEIBER,
MIKE STOLLER and DOC POMUS

BYE BYE, LOVE

Words and Music by FELICE BRYANT
and BOUDLEAUX BRYANT

Moderately fast

SUSIE-Q

Words and Music by D. HAWKINS,
S.J. LEWIS and F. BROADWATER

HAPPY, HAPPY BIRTHDAY BABY

Words and Music by MARGO SYLVIA
and GILBERT LOPEZ

WAKE UP, LITTLE SUSIE

Words and Music by BOUDLEAUX BRYANT
and FELICE BRYANT

Rock Tempo

LITTLE BITTY PRETTY ONE

Words and Music by
ROBERT BYRD

PEGGY SUE

Words and Music by JERRY ALLISON,
NORMAN PETTY and BUDDY HOLLY

NOT FADE AWAY

Moderately bright

Words and Music by CHARLES HARDIN
and NORMAN PETTY

Well, I'm gon-na tell you how it's gon-na be.___
My love is big-ger than a Ca-dil-lac.___

You're gon-na give your lov-in' to me.___
I try to love you but you drive___ me back.___

love to last___ more than one day.___
Your love for me has got to be real___

AT THE HOP

Words and Music by ARTHUR SINGER,
JOHN MADARA and DAVID WHITE

THE STROLL

With a moderately strong rock beat

Words and Music by CLYDE OTIS
and NANCY LEE

Come, let's stroll,_____ stroll a-cross the floor____

Come, let's stroll,_____ stroll a-cross the floor____

Now turn a-round, ba - by,

GREAT BALLS OF FIRE

Words and Music by OTIS BLACKWELL
and JACK HAMMER

GET A JOB

Words and Music by
THE SILHOUETTES

Moderately, with a rockin' beat

Sha da da da, sha da da da da, Sha da da da, sha da da da da, Sha da da da, sha da da da da, Sha da da da,

After breakfast, ev - 'ry day, she throws the want ads right my way and nev - er fails to say, get a job, Sha da da da, sha da da da da, Sha da da da, sha da da da da, Sha da da da,

that I nev - er could find. Sha da da da, sha da da da da,

Sha da da da, sha da da da da, Sha da da da,

sha da da da da, Sha da da da, sha da da da da,

Yip yip yip yip yip yip yip yip, Mum mum mum mum mum mum, Get a

TEQUILA

By CHUCK RIO

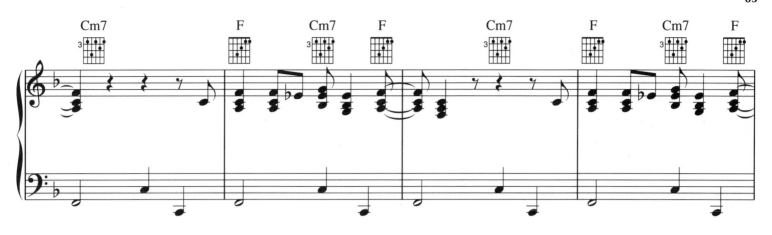

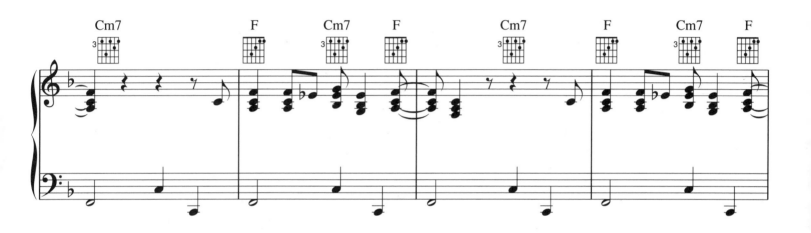

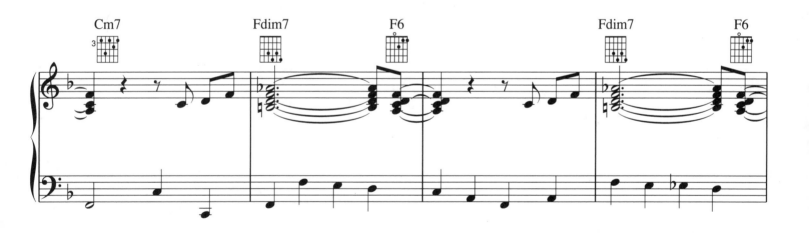

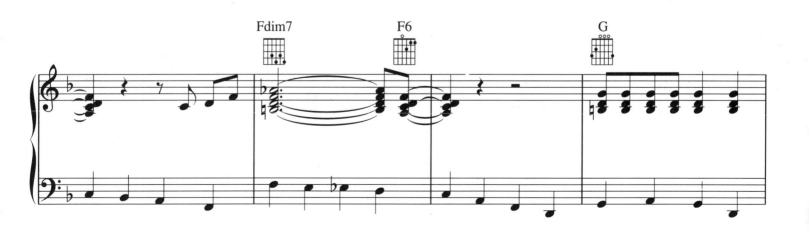

LOLLIPOP

Words and Music by BEVERLY ROSS
and JULIUS DIXON

MAYBE BABY

Moderate Country beat

Words and Music by NORMAN PETTY
and CHARLES HARDIN

May-be, ba-by, I'll have you.___ May-be ba-by, you'll be true.___

May-be, ba-by, I'll have you___ for me.___

It's fun-ny, hon-ey; you don't care.___ You nev-er lis-ten to my prayer.___

Instrumental

ROCK AND ROLL IS HERE TO STAY

Words and Music by
DAVID WHITE

BOOK OF LOVE

Words and Music by WARREN DAVIS,
GEORGE MALONE AND CHARLES PATRICK

TWILIGHT TIME

Lyric by BUCK RAM
Music by MORTY NEVINS & AL NEVINS

ALL I HAVE TO DO IS DREAM

By BOUDLEAUX BRYANT

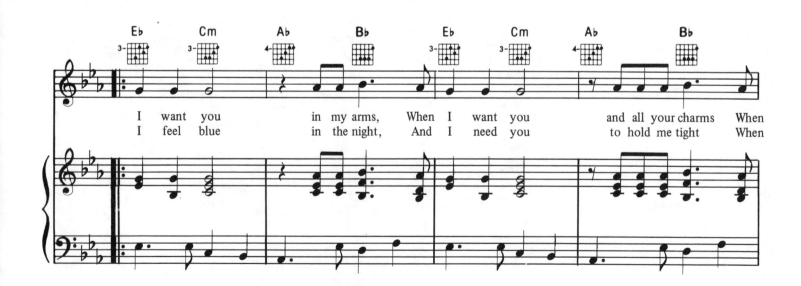

DO YOU WANT TO DANCE?

Words and Music by
ROBERT FREEMAN

PURPLE PEOPLE EATER

Words and Music by
SHEB WOOLEY

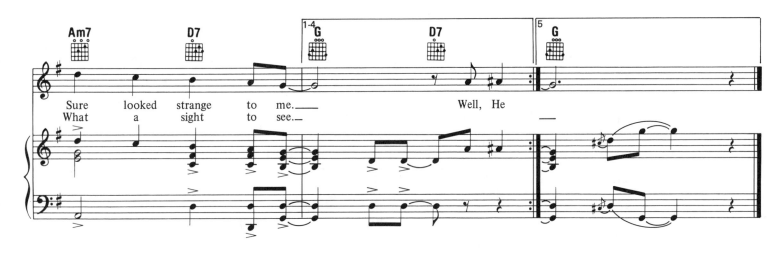

3. I said, "Mister purple people eater, what's your line?"
   He said, "Eatin' purple people, and it sure is fine,
   But that's not the reason that I came to land,
   I wanna get a job in a rock and roll band."

4. And then he swung from the tree and he lit on the ground,
   And he started to rock, a-really rockin' around.
   It was a crazy ditty with a swingin' tune,
   Singa bop bapa loop a lap a loom bam boom.

5. Well he went on his way and then what-a you know,
   I saw him last night on a T.V. show.
   He was blowin' it out, really knockin' 'em dead.

FOR YOUR PRECIOUS LOVE

Words and Music by ARTHUR BROOKS,
RICHARD BROOKS and JERRY BUTLER

SPLISH SPLASH

Moderately, with a beat

Words and Music by BOBBY DARIN
and JEAN MURRAY

WILLIE AND THE HAND JIVE

Words and Music by
JOHNNY OTIS

Bright Rock tempo

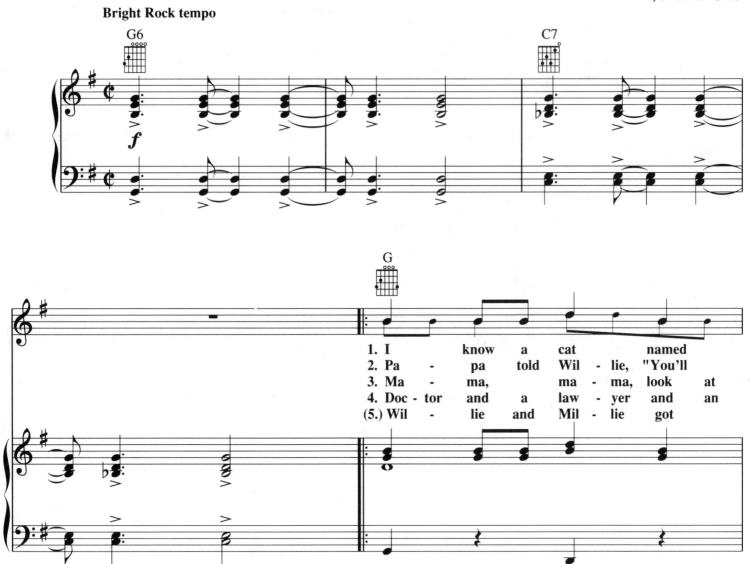

1. I know a cat named Way - Out Wil - lie. He got a
2. Pa - pa told Wil - lie, "You'll ru - in my home. He's
3. Ma - ma, ma - ma, look at Un - cle Joe. Now
4. Doc - tor and a law - yer and an In - dian chief. They had a
(5.) Wil - lie and Mil - lie got mar - ried last fall.

REBEL 'ROUSER

By DUANE EDDY
and LEE HAZLEWOOD

Moderately Bright

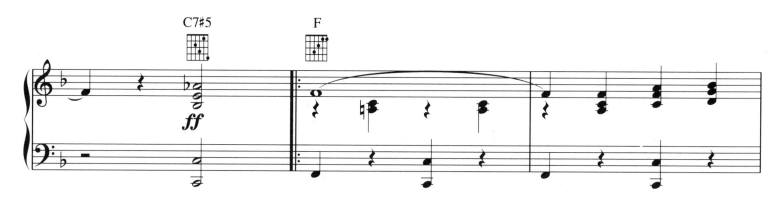

YAKETY YAK

Words and Music by JERRY LEIBER
and MIKE STOLLER

1. Take out the pa - pers and the trash,
2. (Just fin - ish clean - ing up your) room.
3. (You just put on your coat and) hat.
4. (Don't you give me no dirt - y) looks.

or you don't get no spend - ing cash.
Let's see that dust fly with that broom.
And walk your - self to the laun - dry - mat.
Your fa - ther's hip; he knows what cooks.

CHANTILLY LACE

Moderate Boogie Woogie

Words and Music by
J.P. RICHARDSON

TEARS ON MY PILLOW

Words and Music by SYLVESTOR BRADFORD
and AL LEWIS

SUMMERTIME BLUES

Words and Music by EDDIE COCHRAN
and JERRY CAPEHART

BIRD DOG

By BOUDLEAUX BRYANT

VERSE

Johnny is a joker Spoken: (He's a bird) A very funny joker

(He's a bird) But when he jokes my honey (He's a dog) His

jokin' ain't so funny (What a dog) Johnny is the joker that's a

VERSE

2. Johnny sings a love song *(Like a bird)*
   He sings the sweetest love song *(You ever heard)*
   But when he sings to my gal *(What a howl)*
   To me he's just a wolf dog *(On the prowl)*
   Johnny wants to fly away and puppy love my baby *(He's a bird dog)*
   (CHORUS)

3. Johnny kissed the teacher *(He's a bird)*
   He tiptoed up to reach her *(He's a bird)*
   Well, he's the teacher's pet now *(He's a dog)*
   What he wants he can get now *(What a dog)*
   He even made the teacher let him sit next to my baby. *(He's a bird dog)*
   (CHORUS)

ROCKIN' ROBIN

Words and Music by
J. THOMAS

WESTERN MOVIES

Words and Music by FRED SMITH
and CLIFF GOLDSMITH

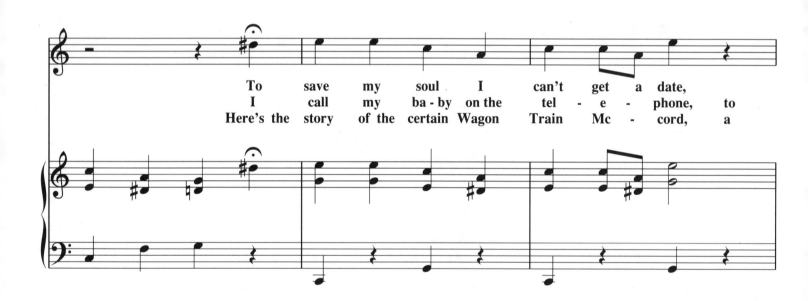

To save my soul I can't get a date,
I call my ba - by on the tel - e - phone, to
Here's the story of the certain Wagon Train Mc - cord, a

ba - by's got it tuned on chan - nel eight, now Wy - att Earp and the
tell her half my head was gone, I just got hit by a
bro - ken arrow has broken my heart, a Jeffer - son Thomas with

CHARLIE BROWN

Words and Music by JERRY LEIBER
and MIKE STOLLER

LONELY TEARDROPS

By BERRY GORDY, JR., GWENDOLYN GORDY
and TYRAN CARLO

SIXTEEN CANDLES

Words and Music by LUTHER DIXON
and ALLYSON R. KHENT

Six-teen can-dles make a love-ly sight But not as bright as your eyes to-night. Blow out the can-dles, Make your wish come true For I'll be wish-ing that you love me

VENUS

Words and Music by
ED MARSHALL

GUITAR BOOGIE SHUFFLE

By ARTHUR SMITH

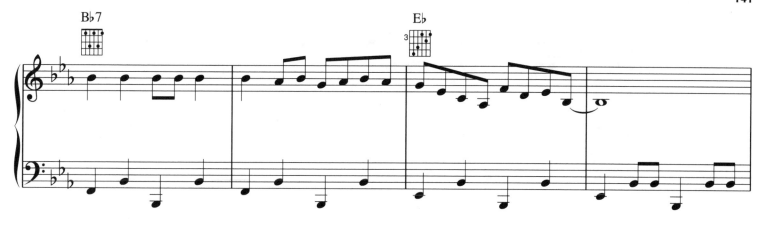

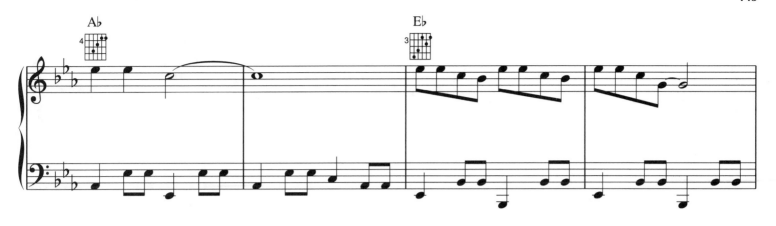

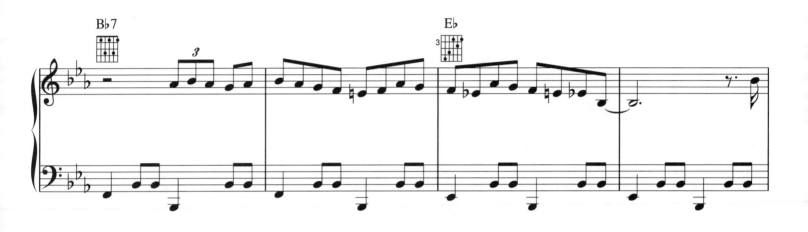

TURN ME LOOSE

Words and Music by DOC POMUS
and MORT SHUMAN

Lyrics:

Turn me loose, turn me loose, I say, — This is the first time I ev-er felt this way. Gon-na get a thou-sand kicks, gon-na kiss a thou-sand chicks, So turn me loose.

Turn me loose, turn me

A TEENAGER IN LOVE

Words and Music by DOC POMUS
and MORT SHUMAN

(YOU'VE GOT) PERSONALITY

Words and Music by HAROLD LOGAN
and LLOYD PRICE

LIPSTICK ON YOUR COLLAR

Moderate rock beat

Words by EDNA LEWIS
Music by GEORGE GOEHRING

LONELY BOY

Words and Music by
PAUL ANKA

SEA OF LOVE

Words and Music by GEORGE KHOURY
and PHILIP BAPTISTE

WHAT'D I SAY

Words and Music by RAY CHARLES

RED RIVER ROCK

Words and Music by TOM KING,
FRED MENDELSOHN and IRA MACK

POISON IVY

Words and Music by JERRY LIEBER
and MIKE STOLLER

WHITE LIGHTNING

Words and Music by
J.P. RICHARDSON

THE MOST DEFINITIVE SET OF ROCK SONGBOOKS EVER PUBLISHED! EACH BOOK CONTAINS OVER 30 BIG HITS ARRANGED FOR PIANO, VOICE AND GUITAR, AS WELL AS A DETAILED ROCK HISTORY OF THE TIMES – COMPLETE WITH PHOTOS AND CHART RECORDS OF THE SONGS. EVERY ROCK HISTORIAN AND FAN WILL WANT TO MAKE THIS SERIES PART OF THEIR COLLECTION!

BIRTH OF ROCK AND ROLL

This first volume explores rock's rhythm and blues roots and its earliest tunes – from "Rocket '88" and "Shake, Rattle And Roll" to the major hits of Elvis Presley, Little Richard, Jerry Lee Lewis, Buddy Holly, and more.

Song highlights include: All Shook Up • Blueberry Hill • Blue Suede Shoes • Earth Angel • Heartbreak Hotel • Long Tall Sally • Lucille • Goodnight, It's Time To Go • The Green Door • Rock Around The Clock • Tutti-Frutti • and more! 00490216/$12.95

THE HISTORY OF ROCK
THE DEFINITIVE ROCK & ROLL SERIES

THE LATE '50 S

The declaration "Rock And Roll Is Here To Stay" led the way for American Bandstand greats like Paul Anka, Frankie Avalon, Fabian, Bobby Darin, and Connie Francis. This book also explores the novelty song hits, the close harmony styles, and romantic ballads that filled the radio waves.

Song highlights include: At The Hop • Chantilly Lace • Do You Want To Dance? • Great Balls Of Fire • Lollipop • Rock And Roll Is Here To Stay • Sea Of Love • Splish Splash • Tears On My Pillow • Tequila • Wake Up, Little Susie • Yakety Yak • and more. 00490321/$14.95

For more information see your local music dealer or contact:

HL Hal Leonard Publishing Corporation
7777 West Bluemound Road P.O. Box 13819 Milwaukee, WI 53213

Prices, availability and contents subject to change without notice

THE EARLY '60 S

Surf music, doo wop, and dance crazes set the stage for a new decade. This volume explores the success of the Beach Boys, "Big Girls Don't Cry," and the Twist.

Song highlights include: Barbara Ann • Breaking Up Is Hard To Do • Do Wah Diddy Diddy • Duke Of Earl • Hit The Road, Jack • Louie, Louie • My Boyfriend's Back • Runaway • Sherry • Surfin' U.S.A. • Tell Laura I Love Her • The Twist • Under The Boardwalk • Wooly Bully • and more. 00490322/$14.95

THE MID '60 S

The British invaded the charts and Hendrix re-invented the guitar in this volume, featuring chart toppers of the Beatles, the Moody Blues, the Hollies, Rolling Stones, Mamas and Papas, James Brown, the Byrds, and many more.

Song highlights include: All Day And All Of The Night • California Dreamin' • Can't Buy Me Love • Dedicated To The One I Love • For Your Love • Gloria • Groovin' • Help! • Hey Joe • I Want To Hold Your Hand • Papa's Got A Brand New Bag • Summer In The City • Wild Thing • Yesterday • and more. 00490581/$14.95

THE LATE '60 S

The turbulence of this era created a new mood for rock and roll. From the classic "Sgt. Pepper's Lonely Hearts Club Band" to the San Francisco sound to Janis Joplin to the jazz/rock hits of Blood, Sweat and Tears, you'll find the songs that made the statements of the time in this volume.

Song highlights: Abraham, Martin And John • And When I Die • Born To Be Wild • Come Together • Hey Jude • Incense And Peppermints • The Letter • The Magic Bus • San Francisco (Be Sure To Some Wear Flowers In Your Hair) • Spinning Wheel • The Sunshine Of Your Love • White Room • A Whiter Shade Of Pale. 00311505/$12.95